73

Here I Am Burn Me

CঙЗ

by Kimberly Nguyen

Write Bloody Publishing

writebloody.com

First edition.
ISBN: 978-1949342444

Cover Design by Derrick C. Brown
Interior Layout by Write Bloody Publishing
Edited by Sam Preminger
Proofread by Wess Mongo Jolley
Author Photo by Beowulf Sheehan

Type set in Crimson.

Printed in the USA

Write Bloody Publishing
Los Angeles, CA

Support Independent Presses
writebloody.com

to my ancestors,
who did the best they could.
and to my descendants,
for whom i will do better.

Here I Am Burn Me

CONTENTS

This is so you know the sound
of someone who loves you from the ground.
Tonight you're not alone at all.
This is me sending out my satellite call.

— Sara Bareilles, "Satellite Call"

LET ME BEGIN BY WASHING MY HANDS

"are you going to write a poem about it?"

reader, don't blame me: i was born in the starless night.
in the darkness, i saw a shadow and shined a light on it.
and now each star in the sky is a word that i placed,
each star—a pin on the map of my tongue. to name
something is to lift its veil, to drag it from the depths
of the cloudy water to the surface. to name something is
to know it. i never once wrote a single word out of spite;
i wrote a path out of the darkness. i'm sorry to everyone
my path cut through, but i named every place i ran into.
every poem i've ever written was not made; it was
already there. and this is the way the universe was
built. matter is neither destroyed nor created,
just transferred. every word you say to me, i send
back. i set free. the further i tunnel through the dark
the more i understand my life's work is not mine.
my tongue—the surface of a lake. the lake—my body
of work. you look down into the murkiness, wanting
to know its depth, and see your own face staring back.

Satellite Call: Hermes

from: me
to: home

hello? is anyone there? can you hear me?
if you can hear me, can you point me
towards our solar system? i shot
for the moon, misfired, and lost myself
in this galaxy. i am looking for a way home.
in my first language, the word for "home"
can sometimes mean "family." the tongue
that blurs that line is the same one that smudges
the ink in my name. we recreate our first wounds
in order to change the ending. in my first life, i died
smeared under the boot of a soldier, limb
indistinguishable from other limb, wing
from other wing, so the gods scattered
each piece of me into a separate new life.
it's taken me all of human history to understand
what i have been looking for: home—
that first wound that broke me into a yearning
creature. each of my lives—that wound's recreation,
the bitter hope that this iteration will be
different, that it will be another ending.

A Vietnamese Coming-Home Greeting

thưa mẹ con mới về

về   a verb   i have not used   in five years.

        what is home   but a place   a mother calls you?

        but i have pressed my ear against the cold glass telephone

        and nothing.

i am a daughter   which means i was born writing

                                    poems out of absence.

     absence   a language without words   instead graveyards
                      with all the holes dug   and no bodies.

let me show you, mẹ.

mẹ—mother/ me—myself/ i am—the absence of a diacritic/   an error.

nếu con là con thuyền   mẹ là mặt trăng chiếu trên nước sông
    if i am a boat mother, you are the reflection of the moon on the river.

i am gliding across the black night   to touch you   //i will never reach
you

i am going the wrong way i am the boat but i am also the water,
a mirror.

reflection   a language of refractions   you look down and see yourself:
a daughter

and the distance between—an absence.

No, Where are You Really From

because my father says   i came to him in a fever dream

     that homesick, he closed his eyes   and tasted eden

his tongue split   open

       and from the folds   i emerged.

in another version of the story   i am a reincarnation   an unfulfilled life

a raindrop   that never reached the bottom of the mountain

before the earth swallowed it.   in an old myth   i am delivered by

either the waves or the shore   depending on the translation.

but in the true version of the story, i was salt.
     i would know.   i was there.   i remember.

i calcified into bone	i became the rib of a fish
that my father caught and	brought to my mother
that my mother cooked	and set out for dinner
midway through the meal	i caught in her throat
before i was bone	before i was salt
i was an ion	waiting to get caught somewhere
aren't we all	waiting to get caught somewhere
my mother coughed and coughed	[a swallowed bone passes
from this iteration	to the next]
in one final hack	she expelled me
pulled me out	put me down.

ARS POETICA

a dive   is a prayer that breaks   water   my body—a violence
that pierces the ocean   my body—seventy percent water   and still
the furthest state from it   as deep as i dive   into the starless abyss
i will always be   a displacement   and never water.

water—   the closest resemblance to a womb.   language—
the difference between me   and this body of water.   in reckless hope
i'll try to drown myself   swallow my volume in seawater   believe
that if i consume the difference   i'll eradicate it.   i come parched;
i leave gasping,   the answers   buried   in the deepest
point of my body   the center of a vortex   that refuses to swallow
me.

i roll stones   up the crest of a wave;   they all fall through.
i eat and eat   the flesh of a fruit and never reach the seed,
the distance from the center   equal to the span of my desire.   there is
no destination in this art—   only approximation   the way water
molecules   cannot atomically touch me,   but i know when i've been
submerged.

ON BEING CHỊ HAI (VERSE 1)

i am the eldest daughter[1] of an eldest daughter of an eldest daughter.

---

[1]   see also: *surrogate mother.* the fraying thread my family hangs by. before my mother was a daughter, she was a mother to her mother. needing a mother, she created the next best thing: a daughter. and now i'm afraid to leave my sisters motherless. four daughters in a house made of orphan lines.

WRITING IS ALWAYS A POLITICAL ACT

to write my name
is to crucify myself on paper.
it is to say
here
i am.
        burn me.

PLANETARY ALIGNMENTS

i don't know much about love,
but i do know i almost grazed
by it. before i came to this corner
of the galaxy, i was the moon
of another planet, spun out of orbit
by weak gravity. weak gravity—
the only gravity i'd ever known.
i was always a temporary celestial body,
spinning in and out of orbits too weak
to hold me, grasping at the air
trying to hold myself in place.

facing the wrong direction, i almost missed
you. mourning what could have been,
those other planets and what i imagined for us,
i turned my dark side to what was. that night,
i almost didn't come to the restaurant,
almost reached into my closet for an excuse
instead of my favorite skirt, almost ordered in
instead of a drink. in an alternate universe,
i don't invite you home to meet my dog
after you tell me about yours, the sun
doesn't rise on us still laughing on the couch,
and there is nothing for you to come back for.

you caught me by surprise, veered me
off my original course, intercepted me
with the strongest center of gravity
i had ever felt. yanking me
into your atmosphere, you transformed me
from moon to meteor. i've forgotten
what i was looking for before i crash
landed on you. all i want to know now
is how big a crater my landing left on you.

SATELLITE CALL: EARTH

from: me
to   mẹ

hello? mẹ? can you hear me?
if you can hear me, can you
send me a sign? i heard it
takes light over five hours to reach
pluto from the sun. i am out here
in orbit further away. can you reach
me? the farther i get, the fuller
the picture of us i see, but the fuller
the picture i see, the less i can tell
if you love me. mẹ, are you there?
i am firing all my distress calls
to you. sos. can you hear me?
do you love me?

WHAT I MEAN WHEN I SAY THE WAR IS STILL HERE

my family is not made of war;
we are made of craters.

a bomb exploded and broke
the earth; its dust flew up and cut
the air, and what did we have left
but wounded atmosphere?

i often say my childhood was a war zone;
what's the difference between war and its aftermath
when the dust settles back in its place
and at the first drop of the sour rain?
how it all returned to itself, ash to ash
dust to dust, as if nothing had changed.

what then do we know of endings
if the morning still comes again?

I LOVE YOU THE WAY ONLY A CHỊ HAI COULD

without bounds. without boundaries. selflessly. and i mean i'll love you like i have no self to love. in my family, i am all the good adjectives: giỏi, ngoan, hiền. every girl in my family wants to be good, obedient, and meek. by that definition i am a "good" girl, born a trophy daughter, becomes a trophy wife. whatever you want, i'll be her. i'll be a one-line poem you take a black marker to, black out all the parts of me you don't want to see. i'll be a one-line poem in a font so small you might mistake me for a blank page. i'll be the centerpiece of the dinner table, the accent piece, the girl you take out for the guests and put away when the guests go home. i'll be a blessing and miracle and you'll be lucky to have me. i'm the girl everyone bends into a girl they're lucky to have. all the guests will jokingly ask where they can get one of me as they walk to their cars and you'll laugh and say they can borrow me. and tell me it isn't true. tell me you aren't lucky. tell me what more you could want in a room for two that you'll get all to yourself.

EXPLAINING DEPRESSION TO MY FAMILY

i apologize
          for this uneven road i am laying
                    as i stitch these words onto the page
                              with a broken sewing machine.

my mother tongue is a love letter
          with the text half redacted,
                    an erasure
                    i am rearranging
                              to lure out of reach language
                                        into my grasp.
          i typed "serotonin" into google translate
and couldn't find it there either.
                    my dictionary is a long list
                              of death certificates
                                        and ripped stitches.

what i am trying to say
          is some days the sky is gray for no reason.
                    you can love a plant and it can still wilt away.
                              you turn on all the lights
          and a dark vignette still sits in all four corners of the room.
you know how sometimes in deep fever
                    your body burns but all you feel is cold?

all i touch is cold   all my life—a blue flame.

A FIRE THAT BURNS TWICE AS BRIGHT

burns half as long.[1]

---

[1]   only if we let it burn out.

once in chemistry class, i pumped hydrogen into soapy water, gathered the suds into my hands, and set them ablaze. and the hydrogen burned away so fast the flame never touched my hands. you are building a wall like this around your heart, hoping that you might leave this love un-scorched. you are balancing these chemical equations trying to find an answer so you might predict the ending, but you are forgetting how this all began. in the beginning—the big bang—all the atoms that make up you and me were already created. and those atoms have travelled 13.8 billion years to be here and have now led me to you. the big bang lasted 10^{32} seconds which means it lasted .00000000000000000 000000000000001 of a second and we are still here. so let the evidence show that this explosion did not die out; it only grew. you are right to be afraid that a fire that burns twice as bright burns half as long, but our story is already doomed to be a brilliant flash that dies quickly. our whole lives will span 100 out of 13.8 billion years—a quarter of it already gone. that's barely a blink of the universe's eye. i want you to burn with me. come see what size star we can become before we collapse. come believing that the fires that burn twice as bright are the only ones worth starting.

ON BEING CHỊ HAI (VERSE 2)

i am the eldest daughter of an eldest daughter[1] of an eldest daughter.

---

[1] see also: translator. between motherland—immigrant—new country. by the transitive property, the tongue—a rubber band stretched thin. the daughter on the phone with the insurance company, ordering the pizza, calling the bank, chasing away the door-to-door evangelists, the cable tv salesmen. the first grader sounding out stock market vocabulary, reading my mother the money section of the sunday paper. what do i send you to school for, she cries at my faltering syllables. "translate" is from a latin root that means "to be carried across." i am sent, a dutiful guard to a watchtower, to discover and pass down in reverse a language neither of us has ever known, to fortify this family for what i can see coming in the tower distance. the hand strikes me, and i do not pay it forward. the words come to me as weapons, and i disassemble them to build homes from the scrap metal. but now my life is a barren wasteland of haunted houses that i'll spend the rest of my life trying to put back into words.

LONGING FOR NEBRASKA

i point across the ocean.

                    i name it   home.

my mother spins me around   *that's not your home.*

        my finger falls on a burning field   *there,*

that's home.

so i must live in a house of ash then—

            once i came to school covered in ash

            and my teacher brushed me off.

            i am always asked to take the high road

            that i must build myself, and now i'm here   alone.

i just want to live somewhere where i can be prom queen.

i want a home where i can cover myself in glitter.

i am trying to teach my mother the word   salvageable   like

      how nothing in this home   is salvageable.

      we've gathered   all the pieces we want to save

      into urns;   they just become new vessels   for our grief.

forgive me, i left out of spite   not for the place, but for myself;

i could not perform miracles.   i tried and i tried and the ash remained

ash.   i prayed and i prayed   but could not return

to my original state.   i am always trying to return everything

to its original state   return ash to itself before the flames.   i am

tracing lineage back to the sea, where the line breaks.   my life has

transformed   beyond the threshold   my two hands

can carry it back to.   believe me when i say   i never leave

any place just to leave it,   when i say   i am trying to return

to the ash   to build for these floating remains   flesh bodies

but the past denies itself the present.   i build a body and get an urn.

i am up to my chest   in cold porcelain   and i feel it

too, my bones—on their way to fire   my skin—in the next life

an urn   a new vessel.   i see my body   from a distance

an unceasing transfiguration   by the fire.   we are changed

beyond recognition   flame—a doorway i have walked through

and can't return to.   in the frame   i see my body

from a distance   a kiln, firing up.

THE AX FORGETS/THE TREE REMEMBERS

mother

i need you to know that despite you
i became a forest. this is just the way
evolution goes: i was born wanting

to survive. i regenerated faster than you
could sever off my branches; each incision
became a brand new tree, firmly rooted.

war deforested you, so you planted
me to see what you could keep alive.
you took cuttings of me hoping to revive

yourself, to wield in your own two hands
the same agent (orange) that once took
your agency. sustained for that purpose, i stood

no chance. i bled and bled but am i
not still here? did i not survive you?
mother, read this again and again:

i was hurt and this is my memory. i will tell
this story until you remember it, until you've learned
your own disaster by heart. there's no other side

of this story, only the sharp side of your tongue.
mother, i cannot forgive you for the wrong
you have not done. you did the only thing you knew

how to do. you swung only to find
a solid place: the air parts for the ax; my body
stops it. what does it matter anymore? it is done.

it is done, and i am still here.

CON HƠN CHA NHÀ CÓ PHƯỚC

father   the saying goes   that if your child climbs higher than you
the whole family is fortunate.

                    every night, you lifted   me and my sister
onto your two shoulders   and carried us up the stairs to bed.
even when i grew too old   you still knelt   at the bottom of the stairs
so i could climb your back towards the sky.

opportunity: from an old latin phrase   that means coming towards a port,
how standing on the dock,   you realized that once a boat came for you,
and you took it to this country;   that was the furthest it would go.

the saying goes   when your child climbs higher than you
you should feel the blessing   coursing through the family bloodline,
but what they don't tell you   is that when you send her away
she will go   where you cannot follow her.   and what is
there left for you?

a father's love   is many things,   but it is not perfect.
you gave your whole life   so i could surpass you   gave me all you could
not have   and now you see me in the stars: a blessing
and also a cruelty   a joy   and a resentment.   your grief
that one day you woke up   still standing on the dock
and didn't realize what had passed: that your daughter
once a weight upon your back   is now a stranger in the distance
and you cannot say   which of the two you love more.

AN OBJECT AT REST

stays at rest   unless acted upon by a force.
    i don't know if we are   the right ones for each other
but we are both our own   force. when we move
    together, we shoot through space   so fast, time itself warps
around us. i barely blinked   and now there's a toothbrush
    on my counter and your clothes   in my closet. i know
the cost of the space   i am making for you, that what is today
    the shape of you could tomorrow   be the absence of you.
when we both pull away   we pull so hard, time stops
    and starts turning the other way.   an object in motion
stays in motion   unless acted upon by a force.
    i cannot be a tide   you rock back and forth.
you cannot flood my shore   and then abandon it.
    you cannot keep running   at each cosmic ripple i cause.
if we are in motion,   let fear not be the force
    that stops us.

MY FATHER SAYS HE THOUGHT I WENT TO COLLEGE FOR HIM

i am sorting through — the contents of my life
to determine what is mine — and what is yours
i was just a child — i needed you
to handle my life — with care
i remember the first time — i learned the monstrance is so holy
that our human hands — are unworthy
i am looking for any part of me — that is just as sacred

i understand all your reasons: — you closed your eyes
and your country vanished — you were carried here on a boat
so i was your anchor — you wanted a new life
so you made one — i am here
because you needed me — to be

you said the world was my oyster — you sent me to open it
i bloodied my hands — and you reaped the pearl

but the world i want is the whole ocean

i need you to realize — this life i have
is because you gave it to me — and you can't take it back
in trying to claim my life, you forgot — in this family, we are all ghosts
stealing lives from one another — so i took my life and ran
and now you haunt me — i am asking you earnestly
because you want my life — joy
when i find it — will i get to keep it

MY MOTHER ASKS ME TO COUNT TO 50 WITH HER

1.
the cane breaks ground, and wisterias bloom where the capillaries on my back split open.

2.

this is what i remember: not the cane, not the pain, not my mother's rage.

3.

i saw my grandmother's face, her grandmother's face, those ghostly eyes overlapping.

4.

i count with my mother to mark the cane's cadence, like soldiers count their steps into battle.

5.

where our voices meet, our grandmothers' war cries join the chorus. con hư tại mẹ cháu hư tại bà.

6.

each mother learns from the one before—you can prune a perfect daughter in 50 clippings.

7.

each daughter passes on this art, loving and overpowering with the same shears.

8.

my mother returns to harvest the garden she beat into me.

9.

an orange grove grows across my chest; my mother takes all its fruit.

10.

i learn to hide between my legs; my mother pries them open.

11.

i am trying to see my grandmother's hand in this act, and it vanishes.

12.

there is no ghost of this atrocity—50 hands laid on a resisting body and it's a new war.

13.

i am trying to explain to my family what has happened in my mother tongue.

14.

but my mother has withheld the word for what she's done to me. i spend my life looking for it.

15.

this is the problem with mother tongues.

16.

my mother cut my tongue into hers, but our language is a broken one.

17.

this is also my origin story: i went looking for a word and never stopped.

18.

i write not because i am full of words, but because they keep eluding me.

19.

i learn my mother's language so that i can understand her.

20.

i am tracing through my lineage, the etymology of my pain.

21.

i forgive my mother; this was the only language she had.

22.

the women in my family tell me my mother hurts me because she loves me.

23.

i watch the mothers in my family raise daughters who marry and follow their husbands home.

24.

no wonder we are always wishing for sons; a daughter is not meant to stay.

25.

who is it that says, "when a writer is born into a family, the family is finished"?

26.

i am here. this family is finished.

27.

i am cutting every root of this family tree, snapping every violent branch.

28.

i begin a new dynasty.

29.

mẹ, nước chảy đa mòn. water flows and the rock erodes.

30.

i am the rock and also the water.

31.

i have taught myself a language you cannot count in.

32.

the cane, rendered useless, floats away downstream.

33.

mẹ, let us count to 50 one last time.

34.

by the time we get to 50 you can't hurt me anymore.

35.

in my new language, i have the word for what you did to me.

36.

i am withholding the word from you.

37.

only i need a name for how you hurt me.

38.

to name how you hurt me, you'd have to understand that you hurt me.

39.

i don't have a translation to bridge that gap in your understanding.

40.

in vietnamese, the word for origin is nguồn gốc. nguồn = source, gốc = root.

41.

the root sucked up the poison from the soil, so i suck out the poison from the root.

42.

you raised a daughter to leave you, and so she did.

43.

between us, me, the right words will always elude me.

44.

once, you spoke to me through the end of a cane, and i swallowed each utterance.

45.

i refused to spit the utterance back out.

46.

and this, i understand now, is the art you were trying to teach me: how to silently bear this family's mistakes.

47.

i pulp the cane to turn it into a soft page for words to land.

48.

here i am, spitting these words back out, giving them back.

49.

here i am ending the violence this family began.

50.

here i am: a new tree to lean on.

SATELLITE CALL: JUPITER

from: me
to: ba

hello? ba? can you hear me? if you can
hear me, can you call me to you? mę said
the older i got, the better i would understand
you. the limits of our understanding depend
on our proximities to one another,
and the older i get, the further you drift
away from me. i heard that in defiance
of our predictions, the fabric of space is
expanding and stretching the distance
of everything in it. at every measurement
of time, we are moving further away
from one another. we don't know
what will happen. maybe we all collapse
and start all over. maybe the fabric of space
rips and sends us flying every which dimension.
whatever happens, i hope i'm with you.

EXPLAINING AMERICA TO MY COUSIN

how to say the american dream
    is a gold-woven rug they will pull out
from underneath you. how to say
    i was born destined to die, but this country
will drag out my corpse, that i was
    born only to build my life back into the ground.
whatever you were running from
    run back. this country sold my father a house
with a rotting foundation, and now
    every generation after pays interest on the mortgage.
everything we have is everything we don't.
    a bank owned everything before we could
and we got the secondhand scraps.
    my father told me to climb the ladder.
this country's ladder stands on quicksand.
    you say, but we have you and i am
telling you my life here has limitations
    and you are outside its bounds. don't pray
to me, your american goddess. don't think
    that because i tunneled out first you can
follow. the tunnel collapsed. i didn't make it.
    i know i was born the year of the ox, chosen
because i am the strongest, ordained
    to cross the river and carry the rest
to safety. how to say that i was
    this family's american dream
that this family made me
    its reckless highest hope, but we are
back right where we started:
    still on the wrong side of the river we can't cross,
somewhere i can't save you from.

MY FAMILY TRIES TO CURE MY DEPRESSION

you say i am your happy girl.
you want the life of your party
to stop hiding in the bathroom
and return.
you say the room without me is a ghost town
but believe me when i say
that i am the ghost
patiently waiting for my life to return
from the bathroom.

MY FATHER SAYS HE WOULDN'T RIOT IF THE POLICE KILLED ME

grief—   a word i'm not sure exists in my mother tongue.
when his mother died   my father's words did too   and i understood
then   that this is how we understand grief—   a cavity
in the mouth   with no syllables   teeth floating in saliva
no destination.   no lighthouse survives   here.

the easy answer   is that my father is racist.   he believes that death
can never arrive early   that death is a doorbell you ring yourself
and i could accept this   and get out of the car   before he drives us both
down this road   winding us into wreckage   but the hard answer
is that my father doesn't know what it means   to grieve.
a lifetime of losses   erodes their significance   but i—born a grievance—
am the inheritor of each loss.   all i am is sorrow   and sorry.
i break the cycle and take the wheel.

father   if you lose me   throw every brick that builds our house.
in this country   we are all brown bodies   bleeding in the street;
our blood burns   if you ignite it.   i know i cannot say this
in a language you understand   because i am your grief
that can only be known   in silence.   but what is grief
that doesn't split the sky open   and flood the whole earth?
what is grief   but two tectonic plates protesting   as they break apart?
does the earth not crumble?   does the land not fall   into the sea?
father, this is grief: the way a destination is the difference   between ship
and driftwood.   father, if you lose me   will you not
cross this sea   to find me?

I DROVE YOU HOME FOR THE LAST TIME

my foot trembled on the gas the whole seven hours
we left tire tracks on our memories

i was still coughing up fragments   of grief, denial, and a bad cold
so i took cough drops to soothe the pain   i mistook the numbness
for hope and suppressed each truth   trying to crawl its way out
tried to stop my body   from expelling all its excess
i held my breath until i turned blue   drowned my lungs
because i forgot how to let it out   until it all burst from me   and i lost
my breath on the new jersey turnpike   heading south//

i knew this was goodbye   though we said see you later   i tied
all our sentences together   so there would be no endings   i should've said
i love you   but i set my breath free   and it never came back
to be honest,   you should've known   should've figured it out
after we had unpacked all the boxes   had made your new bed
and laid in it   covered ourselves with dust   and all we left unsaid
and both of us,   afraid to kick it up into the air again
afraid to make a cloud   that would pour honest rain   let it settle//

ask all the gods   i sent each one so many prayers   i burned
the road map so that its smoke would reach you   i sent you signs
that pointed back to me   i wrapped the smoke around your ankles

                but you know what they say if you love someone//

these days i return to the car   and climb in the backseat   i watch
all the moments before i knew they were final   i take the trip again
and again   watch our two ghosts flicker   an over-loved vhs
cassette fading from overuse   here   i give you
back this memory   it is yours to keep   i don't need i
anymoretonight, i return to the car   and get in the driver's seat
i drop you off, say see you later

turn the key in the ignition
and drive away//

MY FATHER HAS NEVER TAKEN ME TO HIS VILLAGE

he leaves me behind and goes alone/ has an excuse
why i can't go./ he says someday/ although i know
we are running out of somedays./ his bones creak
a little louder each morning;/ sometimes i mistake it
for the sound of a hinge/ on a closing door./ he is
forgetting some of the places he said he wanted
to show me:/ his father's grave/ his mother's grave/
his childhood home/ the path he used to walk to school./
i see him—/ a row of men he is now and has been/
like a man in the blinding light of a projector/ solid
and transparent at once./ exposed/ he offers me
a sip from his glass/ and i always taste the bitterness
he leaves on the rim./ i see him:/ a child always yearning./
in a murky memory he gave me/ i see him:/ destitute/
in the after-smoke of lunar new year firecrackers./
after all the others have gone inside/ he sifts
through the red debris for un-ignited morsels/ to take
home and light for himself./ i see him/ stealing fruit
offerings off ancestral altars./ ancestral offerings—
a practice he loathes to this day./ the dead have had their fill/
but his life dug his grave with hunger./ i know there are
things in that village he will never talk about./ there are ghosts
there that still haunt him./ he leaves me behind and there
grows a distance between us./ he has carried me this far/
now, he goes forward alone./ i know now that leaving is an absence/
but that absence is not always an empty palm./ like moses's mother,
my father cries a river to send me away from him/
so that when he goes, he goes alone./ whatever ghosts
still tethered to his ankles, he takes with him.

MY MOTHER TELLS ME SHE REGRETS HAVING CHILDREN

mother   believe me   i have also imagined for you a life
without me.   in that version of the story,   i return to your womb
to empty it   of all my belongings   and our bloods never cross
this is what you believe   life without me looks like: a home
where you close your eyes   and no one cries to wake you.
remember how you told me   when i was born i did not cry?   i came
to this version of the story   because you asked me to.   when you
birthed me   my lungs in turn delivered you.   did i not gasp
until i'd expelled you from me?   did the nurse not extract you
from my chest cavity?   in the version of the story without me—
the one i admit i pray for sometimes, too—   you sit in the corner of
our house, growing old.   no one plucks your gray hairs from your head
the way you always asked me to.   let me remind you   why you
brought me here: once in a war   you sharpened your tongue
into a blade.   in your sleep, i still see you with a whetstone;
in your wake you cannot help   the way your every word splits me open.
there is no other version of this story;   there is only the one
where you were once   in an empty room   without me
where every harsh word   echoed   and came back to you
when i arrived   didn't my body   stop each blade in its path?
my body—   a soft place for a sharp word to land.   tell me,
didn't i save you from yourself?

CON ĂN CHƯA

yes[1]

---

[1]   don't hang up please hold on. i've been telling all my secrets to a dial tone, replacing you, and now there is a phantom ringing in my ear. who else is a mother but a mother? i know better than to offer what you don't ask for. once, i exceeded all your expectations, and you cut off my excess. so what you don't know is what you don't ask, and what you don't ask is what you don't want to know. i want you to ask. ask me why a pen is a weapon i keep turning on myself. ask me if i'm still cutting myself and why. i was never good at tending wounds. ask me what i am doing about the bleeding. yesterday i almost died from the blood loss, and i wondered if my last word to you would be yes. is this all you want to ask me for the rest of our lives? will that be all you want to know? when i say goodbye, will you tell your secrets to the dial tone? let me tell you what i've learned: it doesn't answer. who else is a daughter but a daughter? you gave me a name so that i would come when you called. once i was a baby crying out for you and you came then. who else is a mother but a mother and who else is a daughter but a daughter? don't hang up. call me back to you.

LOVE IS A HUMBLE EXPRESSION

father   we will be silent when we are dead.   let's not die   here
everyday   your face hardens and grays   like age is pouring
cement into you.   if time does not stop   catching us all by surprise
the next time i speak to you   will be to a headstone.   father
do you remember all the words   i taught you to say?   when you
took a new country   i taught you your name.   i am afraid
one day   i will pick up the phone   and your breath will be empty
on the other end   but that i will still be overflowing.   i know
you are not a person of words;   i know   that silence
is the only language   we both know   the only octave
that sits in both of our keys.   but i don't want to long   for you
anymore.   i don't want to hear you   only as a yearning
i never satisfy.

i know now what i long for is not you: it is me   in place of you
my words   in your baritone.   i am trying so hard to unstrangle my voice
from your throat   to let silence take up the space between us
without my voice   interceding.   father   do you remember
in church   at the end of the *our father*   you squeezed my hand
before you let it go?   i felt the silence then   so gentle
i almost missed it.   i know now   that you grabbing my hand
tighter   is not control   but the beginning of a release.   so here i am
in the palm of your hand   my newborn hand   wrapped tightly around
your finger.   and i'm asking you to hold me   to release me.

MY PARENTS ASK ME WHEN I'M MOVING BACK

violence is not a language
    we were born with. you were
taught at the hand of another

    hand; the home you knew exploded
and you passed that memory
    down to me. so my first language

was a broken one. i loved you
    in the only way i knew how,
in the only language i knew—

    the one you gave me. if you did not
feel my love, it is because i did not feel
    yours. my love and my language—

merely a mirror of all i'd known.
    i don't blame you, but i owed
it to myself to learn a new language.

    violence—the only vocabulary i knew
how to love with was the same
    i used to describe myself. you saw

the lines on my wrist, gathered
    into uniform stanzas. i made my whole body
a poem of destruction against myself.

    i could not live with myself, being
the cause of my own pain.
    so i left you. away from you, every word

i fired from my lips was a blank round.
    my first language, beyond your four walls
incomprehensible. my first language—

cut from the tundra of an ice age.
    so i cast my entire self into the fire
of a new life, let a new language

forge me, let a new language
melt the ice caps off my tongue.
   i was baptized by the fire.

in the center of the flames
   i saw my own eyes, looking back
at me, and for the first time,

   i could hold myself to the light,
to the intense gaze of a looking glass,
   without setting myself ablaze.

mother, father, i cannot return to you
   because i love you, because the love
you know now is the love this new language

   is teaching me how to pass back to you.
my second language—
   still broken sentences and wrong pronunciation.

i am combing through my tongue
   full of budding words, removing
all the profanity. i am writing

   love poems on my body
where i once took a knife
   and made poems of my own pain.

i cannot risk the return.
   i cannot risk the temptation
to run into the arms

   of what is familiar to me.
this is my love poem
   to you. i cannot come to you,

but won't you come to me?
   make yourself a refugee
once more. leave the cold

ruins that you call home.
     leap into the fire where i have
found warmth, where all i know

     is the gentle touch
of a tender tongue.
     help me remove all the thorns

from this garden.
     learn one more language
for me.

SATELLITE CALL: VENUS

from: 1-800-273-8255
to: me

hello, thank you for calling
the national crisis hotline.
how can i help? can you
hear me? are you there?
if you can hear me, can you
tell me, are you safe? are you
okay? can you tell me what
is going on? do you need me
to send someone? is there anyone
there who can help you? i can help
you. i promise i will not hang up
until you are ready to let go,
until you are safe. it may not
get better, but you will get better.
are you there? i am here. even if
no one else is, i am listening.
i can hear you.

SATELLITE CALL: MARS

from: 1-800-273-8255
to: me

hello, can you hear me? if you can
hear me, send me a vital sign. my heart
is so heavy it's sunk into my foot
and my whole body is trying to go down
with it. i heard once that drowning
is the most painful way to die, that the body
feels each cell pass away—a row of string lights
going out one bulb at a time. sometimes, living
feels like that, and i just want to cut the power.
most of my life, i have been the only light
in a very dark room. is anyone else there?
can you see my loneliness? how stark the contrast?

AUTOPSY OF WAR

war   i am   trying to run from you.   i burn sage
trying to banish you   but the smoke curdles at the sight of you.

i went to therapy   and laid on the operating table.   when my therapist
opened me up   she saw tobacco stains on all my organs.
we rummaged   for a part of me   you hadn't smoked out.
we defused land mines   you had buried and forgotten,   and all
that remained of me was   a skeleton.

i put my organs in jars on a shelf,   and i walk past them every morning.
what is grief but a body that cannot be laid to rest   jars on life support?
what is grief   but the cruelty   dust buries
everything   i cannot bear to?

war   i am   because you were   who am i
if you are not? you have beaten all of my utterances   into ghost notes
but i can't play songs   without them.   will i always be
a placeholder   for a silence?   will i always be
bones   collecting dust?

war   to throw the jars away   i must begin to acknowledge their loss;
i must perform my own autopsy.   i don't want to keep my organs here
but i don't want to let my organs go.   what i really want is whole organs
undamaged organs.   grief   is not the needle
sewing my hollow body back up   but each stitch i keep ripping out.
war   you are my cause of death   and if i am a ghost of you
then i am my cause of death.   whose fault is that, but mine?
whose fault is that, but yours?

MY FRIEND AND I SIGN A SUICIDE PACT

we swear on both our lives, now intertwined
that neither of us departs this life without the other;
no one gets left behind, and in this agreement,
we hope our desires to die never meet,
that they always walk down the same street
and just narrowly miss each other.
sometimes, survival is just about the timing.
sometimes, survival is about the skills.
sometimes, it's the way, i hold your hand
to tell you i want to go home now, but you should stay,
how you clutch my hand tighter and swear if i go,
you're coming with me, so i stay a little longer
so you can dance around the room one more time
and later, you'll stay a while longer so i can finish
my conversation and in the end we both stay at the party,
saying, *how bright this room is when you are in it.*

GRIEF MAKES A GHOST OF ME

war   you are a dream   i can't distinguish   from my wake.
the first time   i saw augmented reality   i spun a globe around the table
and when i reached for it   my hands got entangled   on thin
air—although i could've sworn   there was something   there.
war you are   the shard of colored glass   that turns the whole
room orange.   i scrub at the orange   i dig through your aftermath
i destroy whole houses looking   for anything you haven't touched
and then the glass breaks   and my fingerprints are all over the wreckage.

war   is this you   or is this grief   i once had a dry patch
on my scalp   that i picked into a lesion   and now there's a rose garden
blooming   underneath my hair.   i pace circles   dig up roses
and call the holes anything, but graves.   i am a sleepwalking shell
of a habit i cannot break.   i thought it was the dead that could not rest
but then restless, what am i?

I Didn't Do the Reading

what is another shakespearean sonnet
to the songs i hear my dead sing?

the dead—each taken life—a metered
silence—a note that sustains.

the canon—a song echoing on the walls of a crumbling cave.

what i am trying to say is
i did the reading in lục bát.

i climbed a mountain
and saw my tongue in the burning bush.

i see the sonnets now—a row of doors
i drag my feet through.

i am summoned into each room
by an ancestor i can't yet find.

my eyes graze these bygone poems
and they crumble into bones

and somehow i am short of making a whole body.

I DEVELOP A SKIN PICKING DISORDER
content warning: dermatillomania

what are my fingers are looking for?/ my hair—
broken strings from a harp/ plucked and broken
on the floor./ my skin—falling like a layer of fresh snow/
on the counter,/ i collect the snowflakes into a jar/
and tell myself i'm just trying to see the damage./ i say
i'm just trying to measure this blizzard in inches/
when i know these are my artifacts./ each scab—
an amber stag i mount above my fireplace./
what i know about grief/ i learned here/ to bury
and unbury in the same stroke./ each day—a burial
and an excavation./ i dig up the same wounds/
and pretend they're new./ i bury them again
to discover them./ what am i punishing myself for?/
i forgive every infraction against me/ except those
self-inflicted./ tell me/ in the morning when the snow
has settled into banks/ will you know where to find me/
will i?//

MY MOTHER SAYS I CRACK AN EGG LIKE I'M AFRAID TO HURT IT

i know what my two hands can do

because we have the same hands:

when i was younger, i hit my sister

because my mother hit me.

i hit my sister when i hated her

so i thought my mother hated me.

it's been 20 years

and i still see the ghost

of my palm on my sister's face.

it's been 20 years and

i've learned a more tender language.

there are days

sometimes i fail.

my muscle memory still tries to speak

with violence

with bruising blows.

so now, so softly, i crack eggs

sometimes the shell doesn't split.

i make sure i want to break

before i break it.

i spend eons aiming

before i fire and my mother mistakes that

for indecision

not knowing

sometimes, she is the fragile thing

i hold in my two hands.

to love someone is to know

my own tender heart,

to refuse to break something

more fragile than myself.

ON BEING CHỊ HAI (REFRAIN)

i am the eldest daughter[1] of an eldest daughter of an eldest daughter.

---

[1]   see also: *reincarnation.* each reincarnation blessed with the power of each of its past iterations. i am the eldest daughter of an eldest daughter of an eldest daughter, the second generation of a family who bears no sons. my father, once desperate for a son, sent me away and told me never to come back. it is why i draw the maps, why i mark my path with houses. so even if i never want to, even if i must see my corpses littering the path all who come after me will tread on, i can come back. i can come home. i can remember how i got here. and when my spirit leaves me to become the next iteration, she'll remember where to go.

SATELLITE CALL: SATURN

from: me
to   myself

hello? can you hear me? if you can
hear me, can you tell me who i am?
in vietnamese, there is no difference
between the word for "girl" and the word
for "daughter", so i never knew
i could be a girl separate from being
a daughter. the semantics matter.
in one language, i am predicated
by a role in a family. in the other,
another possibility. what is possible?
who am i when i'm not a daughter?
when i am alone?

ON BEING CHỊ HAI (REPRISE)

i am the eldest daughter[1] of an eldest daughter of an eldest daughter

---

[1]   mother, how am i to know if this life is mine? on the first day, god said *let there be light*, and i became. my life was birthed still and i am desperately trying to save it. why are you always pulling the plug while i hold the defibrillator paddles? my life is lying comatose on life support waiting for me to return to her. i was wrong: i thought this was matriarchy, but this is necromancy. for centuries, we have birthed urns to carry our endings, supplanted the same ghost into a new body. you say you gave me life, but you gave me *your* life. here, mother, i'm so sorry. i must return to you this life that you have given me. this life is not mine to keep; let there be light. even if it shines just for me, let there be light.

I Don't Call Cps Because

i am a daughter of diaspora   so i was born believing   the greatest sin
is to break   apart a family.   once, this government
unsoldered a whole country   and now my family is dispersed
like a blood spatter   i'll never stop analyzing   to try to find
the murder weapon.   i was afraid to re-inflict the same injury
believed a family should have the right   to break itself apart on its own.
i thought that protecting myself   from my parents   meant that i
didn't love them   or maybe that they didn't love me
meant that i was siding with the enemy   so i forgave them for
every shortcoming   because war changes your perspective
into a wounded one.   i've learned   you can have the best intentions
and still commit the war crime   the way i did by leaving this house
as it was   kept us all prisoners of this war zone   and i must ask,
who was i protecting   in saving everyone   except myself?
i don't call cps   because to break apart   this family
is to admit how i failed as its mother   to realize too late i should've
never been.   i thought that my own martyrdom   would be the way
to finish what this family started   but i see so clearly now
in the settling dust: shame, a stain on my two hands   that were once
handed a gun   did not unload it   and instead, fired.

RELAPSE

broken harp strings/ cracked symphonies/
    under the weight of snow/ the roof caves in./
i wasn't careful—/ i collected snowflakes—/
    each tiny, inconsequential particle/ a carcass i couldn't bear/
to discard./ now i'm buried beneath an avalanche
    of my own compulsion./ i thought that i would know what i was
searching for when i saw it./ in the bathroom mirror
    i scratched out the silver/ and found my wounded complexion./
i'm ashamed of this mess i've made/ while my mother is screaming/
    at me from the surface of the snowfall/ atop my entombed body.
i am screaming at her to get a shovel./ i make
    no promises/ that i won't find myself here
again/ that i won't spend the rest of my life
    resisting/ my body's urge to bury itself
but i begin afresh/ i learn to climb out
    of my own grave once more/ i push the snow
back in, let the earth heal.

PRAYER

poem
    light me
        with the blaze of my next step.

                i cannot help
      that i was born a snake
that my path would never be
    straight.

      i carved each undulation
    into stone with my underbelly—
i am a crooked creature

    but each crook is mine.
        every inch of that serpentine trail
            skinned a scale off my body.
        the stone turned to fire
    and i ignited.

i regret
    each path that crossed mine
        but i digress
            because i went
        in the only direction i knew how to go.

    i will always be
an exile of the garden;
        i scale its walls
            only to be struck down again.

    god did not make hell;   god made me

so the underworld would know where to go.

SATELLITE CALL: URANUS

from: me
to: the past

hello? can you hear me
in this dimension? i have
travelled through time
and space to tell you nothing
ever dies. nothing disappears.
matter is neither destroyed
nor created, just transferred.
this is why i can never lose
the past, why i keep driving
and driving and it is always
the same distance in the rearview
mirror, how it reflects in the glow
of my headlights, scaring me.
i veer, turn my head. and there
it is, still behind me, smiling
as if it were always there.

THE ONLY STORIES MY MOTHER KNOWS ARE GHOST STORIES

i still see them now: each unfortunate tale   meant to haunt my decisions
mapped out like a path   i'm not meant to follow.   the severed foot
still hopping around the bedroom   looking for its lost body.   a body
that forgave itself   and moved on.   a foot left behind
with nothing to forgive.   forever an open wound   looking for closure.
a reminder   the body is not a guaranteed passage;   it is always
leaving you behind.   age—the body's cruelest departure.
eternity—a train platform the body never leaves.   my mother tells me
these stories   not so i can avoid death   but so that i can safely cross it.
nothing is meant to live forever   but not all things die.   the severed foot
caught in an eternal waiting room   yearning to hear its name
but no one comes for it.   my history—my own severed limb
jammed in a door i can pass through   but never close.

~~6 WOMEN ARE MURDERED/~~MAN MURDERS 6 WOMEN

tell me a story i haven't heard before;   my mother has told me this one.
in all her stories—   a warning: a woman always dies   and that woman
is always me.   she cleaves   a duck apart for congee
splits its breastbone down the middle   says we are human—   we kill
everything we do not know   until we know it   until we are no longer
afraid of the dead.   once, i pinned a frog open on a metal tray   looking
for its heart   and for weeks i could not stop   smelling the formaldehyde
on my hands. i can no longer trust science   and what it knows about me.
my mother also tells me this story: in vietnam
there once was a type of fish   we loved for its meat   and that is to say
what we don't kill to know   we kill to eat.   so we fished the lakes dry:
a whole bloodline shriveled   down our throats   and when the monsoon
season came   only our bloodlust flooded the streets
and this is life.   on one side of the pond   you are the predator
on the other   you are the prey.   here we are
on the other side of the pond.   in this country   you are
always at another man's mercy—   watch your back. say your prayers.
you look through one end of a gun's barrel   and meet its other end.
don't act surprised.   don't pretend my body is not
always the centerpiece of the table.   what this country doesn't cut open
it puts on a plate   and there's not a single person   who hasn't been
a guest   at this feast.

Mẹ ĐÂY

as i see the past, i can see the future. the first time
i felt her kick, i was thirteen. it was the middle
of the night. i awoke, startled to feel her there
but not there, not quite a ghost nor divination.
i heard her voice, unrecognizable yet so familiar
and saw her, a flickering vision before me.
this is how i learned how to heal time, saw
its glowing expanse coiled around my neck.
in my unravelling i felt the hurt i'd felt
before me and the pain i would inflict
because of that loosens its grip.

let me be very clear: i could leave everything
exactly how it is. i could wrap tomorrow
tightly around the same wound and nothing would change.
but in this version of things, i wrap my whole life
around the same coffin nail and sentence
the next generation to death. in this version,
my daughter calls for me to unbury her,
and i don't answer. war rips a hole in time,
and i don't fix it to get to her.

i am here now, un-hammering the nail
from where it snags the past because no one
before me could. i am weaving the pulled threads
back through. i am here because in the story
as i have written it now, somewhere in the future,
this thorn still catches my daughter and she bleeds.
i am here because i have not yet healed the wound;
i will pass it on to her. i could not rewrite the past;
only my mother could and she didn't. now i cry
for her, and she never comes. i understand
that the more i untangle these threads of time,
the more distantly i will hear my daughter's voice,
that if in this version of the story i am the wound,
then i must write her away from me. so i am here,
a progression of the past and a relic of the future.
i am here, answering her call.

NGủ NGON

what i thought i knew about language   i was wrong
forgive me: i once thought home would be
wherever my first language was   but the last night
i laid with you   we were two drops of water
under the blanket   of a dry, yearning tongue
when you asked me   how to say goodnight in vietnamese
i turned my whole body away   a syllable, misfired
into the dark   my first language—an arrow
that once grazed across my face   the sharp edge, leaving a laceration
that became my mouth.   i don't know how to speak
tenderness in my first language   i caught the arrow between my teeth
and now every utterance breaks skin.   i know now
my second language is what saved me   a salve for a split tongue
our first languages   are also sometimes our first wounds
my second language   warm honey on a cold, hard throat
the only language i could say   goodnight and i love you
the only language i could cry in   when you left me
but before that, in the chasm   between my back and your face,
you whispered the softest words   in mandarin—
your first language—   a voice i'll never hear again
i don't know what you said   and i will never need to know
while you slept,   i lifted the words off your lips
on my tongue   all i could taste was their sweetness.

THIS IS A LOVE LETTER

to jasmine rice   and soy sauce   in the ethnic aisle—
to the crisp melting   of duck skin in my mouth;   you taste   the way
america was supposed to taste—   to the ember   traveling down
our burnt prayers   leaving trails of incense ashes   i sweep of
the ancestral altar—   to the ocean   to water—   to passage—
to fish sauce; if you boil it dry   only salt remains   and i remain
a remnant of the dry season heat   the smoke of a fresh gunshot.
to my father's body—   a rubber band   stretching where ends don't
meet.   the space between one end and the other   is the span
of an immigrant's pride.   i am   an immigrant's pride.
look at me—   i open my hands   and i hold origin stories
in the motes of ash   caught inside the lines on my palms.
i am made of what is left behind   in the heat.   they say the volcano
decimates its mountainside;   no living thing survives.
but at the first rain does the ash not run fertile?

RELAPSE AGAIN

once again, i am here   to face the ghosts i brought back to life.
this is my fault and mine alone;   i could not let a dead thing lie.
once a soldier planted a bomb in my family tree   buried each body,
and i could not let them rest in peace.   i set off each unignited bomb
to try to find the source of my pain. i thought i could change the ending.
i thought i could open each past wound and rectify it,   dig up history
and change it.   each one i uncovered broke me again.
i could not see   that my pain was not   an explosive buried
beneath the surface   but the shovel my own two hands
kept sending in to find it;   now there's a war zone   of bomb craters
buried under my hair.

i am teaching myself the art of ignorance.   just because something is
there   does not mean i have to find it;   i promise
someday, i will not write   about bombs anymore.   someday, i will heal
knowing that the past will always be   a buried secret i cannot know,
a broken clock i cannot fix. that what is gone will stay gone. that what dies
i need never bring back.

WRITING THE WILL

mẹ   ba

      when you leave me   what will you leave

me

      i left you for another life   you said

i needed to learn to live   without you

      i have already   mourned   your loss

          grieved   your absence

i have sealed your tomb   placed   your likeness

      on my ancestral altar   arranged

my offerings   in the shape of a letter

      that will never reach you

once you asked me   *when we die*

      what do you want   *the house*

your mother   *'s engagement ring*

      bà ngoại   *'s jade bracelets*

and i could not imagine   how to replace you

      i said   nothing

leave me nothing   i meant it then

      i mean it now   look at me

in an apartment   that costs more than that house

      i have bought all the things i never had

because i never had them   and i am still missing you

      learning that i cannot live   without you

      in your will

please write   that you will

      never leave me   that you are just giving me

a couple things to hold onto   like a promise i'll keep

      until you need them back again

that your absence   is another lesson   i don't yet understand
          please write   that your love for me never picks up
when i call   but that it's just out of town
          leave a message at the beep   it'll get back to me
when it returns.

ON BEING CHỊ HAI (ENCORE)

i am the eldest daughter[1] of an eldest daughter of an eldest daughter

---

1

see matriarch. empress. american queen. a monarch, cut from her cocoon too early and left to die. my family—vagabond remains of a ghost country, diasporic nation without a sovereign. call it primogeniture, but i earned my crown. i saw a throne, bowed to my duty and ascended it. don't get me wrong: every fruit of my labor grew on the branches of my suffering. i have always longed for more tender branches and less bitter fruit. but i did the impossible. i survived everything and nothing survived me. i broke all the cycles that sought to break me, and this is all to say don't bet against me. i was told history is written by the victors; the victors wrote every word before me. a nation waged a war and brought me here to write me into the dust their bombs kick up. a family lost everything in a war and brought me here to recuperate the remains. but i was the bomb not the dust. i did not salvage the past; i rewrote the future. my descendants will write about me. how i fell before i rose. how everything that didn't kill me made me more deadly. how i was given the broken pieces of the empires before me and made the best life i could.

ALL THE HEARTBREAK POEMS

were endings. are still endings. flowers i left at the bottom of tombstones to make believe loss into something pretty. urns i painted to transfer grief into a new body. i still love each love i lost the same way i love the girl i once was, like a star in the distance releasing me in its dying flicker. and i still love each love i lost the same way i love every place i've ever lived: a home that i left when it was time.

to my love now, all these heartbreak poems are dead trees in a forest we will walk through to get home. you will see each ugly branch unfurl and grab at the hems of your clothing. you will read my heartbreak poems and wonder if these trees could ever come back to life. will i rush away to tend its new growth? believe me, there was a time i would've wished for it, would've watered a dead plant praying it back alive. i chained myself to doors left open calling for the past to walk back through. but from there, i never saw you coming. i would've burned this whole forest down to get to you, but you had to cut through all the thicket to get to me.

i once cursed the universe for its rotation, for how it spun all the ones before you away from me. but i see its full orbit now, what needed to collide to bring you here, what needed to get out of the way. i'll never wonder what if ever again, only what now. what to do now that you are here. what to do now with our time together. this is my last heartbreak poem. turn the page. grab a pen. write your name. a new page with the heartbreak buried underneath.

SATELLITE CALL: MESSAGE FAILED

from: me
to: everyone i've ever loved

if i am too late, i am sorry
                    to the both of us. believe me,
i've asked for every miracle.
                    this is how i know there must be
parallel universes existing
                    at the same time. they are stacked
on top of one another
                    in the same space. we walked
toward each other, and
                    never met. i could see you
but never get to you.
                    i tried every door and i couldn't find
yours. i left all my doors
                    open for you and you never found
your way to me. we were
                    in the right place at the wrong time-
line. we stood parallel
                    to each other but never touched.
i want you to know
                    that my love spans all that distance
that love knows no time or place
                    that my universe is so empty without
you. that it will always be
                    a story i never finished writing, a possibility
that we couldn't explore.
                    what cruelty is this—that you can arrive
but never arrive, leave
                    but never leave. my life—forever altered
because once i saw you
                    and spent the rest of it making my way
towards you.

ACKNOWLEDGMENTS

I have always understood writing to be an act of community and communion, and therefore, I am so full of gratitude to every single person who made this collection of poems possible. First and foremost, I would like to thank the following literary magazines and journals, where some of the poems in the collection first appeared:

diaCRITICS: "on being chị hai (verse 1)"; "on being chị hai (refrain)"; "on being chị hai (reprise)"

Frontier Poetry: "~~6 women are murdered/~~man murders 6 women"

Hobart: "an immigrant love letter"

The Minnesota Review: "grief makes a ghost of me"

perhappened mag: "i drove you home for the last time"; "i develop a skin picking disorder

The Journal: "on being chị hai (verse 2)"

For believing in me and giving me the nurturing career push I needed, I'd like to thank all the staff at PEN America involved in the Emerging Voices program, particularly Jared Jackson and Jenn Dees, who along with my fellowship cohort, were my cheerleaders and friends and will be for life.

For holding space for poets who look like me, and for all their programming which has been such an essential part of my growth and belief in my work, I'd like to thank Asian American Writers' Workshop and Kundiman.

For being the best mentor a young poet could ever ask for, I need to thank Paul Tran who saw the potential in my work that I couldn't see and became my very own chị hai. Em yêu chị rất nhiều.

For seeing me and understanding my angst when the road here got too tough, I want to thank Roya Marsh, who kept it real and did everything in her power to uplift me.

Many thanks to my two sisters, Mai and Elizabeth, without whom I would not have had the privilege of being their chị hai. I am the proudest and luckiest eldest sister in the world.

To mẹ and ba, thank you for everything, the good and the bad.

For being my best and oldest friend and growing up with me, I need to thank Lisa, who has witnessed more crying and mental breakdowns than anyone else in my life has. Thank you so much for holding my hand through all the hardest parts of my young adult life and celebrating me in all the good parts.

For their guidance and friendship, I'd like to thank in no particular order:

Charles Arndt, Farida Tcherkassova, Nikolai Firtich, Dan Ungurianu, Michael Joyce, Hua Hsu, Carla Abella Rodriguez, Alex Koo, Ngoc "Seven" Duong, Ha Bui, Evelyn Frick, Elena Schultz, Danielle Isakov, Sara Inoa, Emma Alexandrov, Rick Jansen, Thuy Le, Tung Vu, Sarah Ghazal Ali, John Silk, Willie Loza, and Hiep Dinh.

Thank you to Derrick Brown and the whole Write Bloody family for all their work and for this opportunity. Thank you for believing in this little book of poems.

Finally, thank you to Noah. If all this book does is makes you proud, I will have done enough.

About the Author

Kimberly Nguyen is a Vietnamese-American diaspora poet originally from Omaha, Nebraska but now living in New York City. Her work can be found in diaCRITICS, Hobart, Muzzle Magazine, The Minnesota Review, and others. She was a recipient of a Beatrice Daw Brown Prize, and she was a finalist for Frontier Poetry's 2021 OPEN and New Poets Awards. She was a 2021 Emerging Voices Fellow at PEN America and is currently a 2022-2023 Poetry Coalition Fellow.

Photo: Beowulf Sheehan

www.kimberlynguyenwrites.com

If You Like Kimberly Nguyen, Kimberly Likes...

This Way to the Sugar, Hieu Minh Nguyen ·

Cut to Bloom, Noah Choi Wild

Floating, Brilliant, Gone, Franny Choi

Drive Here and Devastate Me, Megan Falley

No Matter the Wreckage, Sarah Kay

Write Bloody Publishing publishes and promotes great books of poetry every year.

We believe that poetry can change the world for the better. We are an independent press dedicated to quality literature and book design, with an office in Los Angeles, California.

We are grassroots, DIY, diversity power believers. Pull up a good book and join the family.

Support independent authors, artists, and presses.

Want to know more about Write Bloody books, authors, and events?

www.writebloody.com

WRITEBLOODY
QUALITY AMERICAN BOOKS

WRITE BLOODY BOOKS

After the Witch Hunt — Megan Falley

Aim for the Head: An Anthology of Zombie Poetry — Rob Sturma, Editor

Allow The Light: The Lost Poems of Jack McCarthy — Jessica Lohafer, Editor

Amulet — Jason Bayani

Any Psalm You Want — Khary Jackson

Atrophy — Jackson Burgess

Birthday Girl with Possum — Brendan Constantine

The Bones Below — Sierra DeMulder

Born in the Year of the Butterfly Knife — Derrick C. Brown

Bouquet of Red Flags — Taylor Mali

Bring Down the Chandeliers — Tara Hardy

Ceremony for the Choking Ghost — Karen Finneyfrock

A Constellation of Half-Lives — Seema Reza

Counting Descent — Clint Smith

Courage: Daring Poems for Gutsy Girls — Karen Finneyfrock, Mindy Nettifee, & Rachel McKibbens, Editors

Cut to Bloom — Arhm Choi Wild

Dear Future Boyfriend — Cristin O'Keefe Aptowicz

Do Not Bring Him Water — Caitlin Scarano

Don't Smell the Floss — Matty Byloos

Drive Here and Devastate Me — Megan Falley

Drunks and Other Poems of Recovery — Jack McCarthy

The Elephant Engine High Dive Revival — Derrick C. Brown, Editor

Every Little Vanishing — Sheleen McElhinney

Everyone I Love Is a Stranger to Someone — Annelyse Gelman

Everything Is Everything — Cristin O'Keefe Aptowicz

Favorite Daughter — Nancy Huang

The Feather Room — Anis Mojgani

Floating, Brilliant, Gone — Franny Choi

Glitter in the Blood: A Poet's Manifesto for Better, Braver Writing — Mindy Nettifee

Gold That Frames the Mirror — Brandon Melendez

Open Your Mouth like a Bell — Mindy Nettifee

Ordinary Cruelty — Amber Flame

Our Poison Horse — Derrick C. Brown

Over the Anvil We Stretch — Anis Mojgani

Pansy — Andrea Gibson

Pecking Order — Nicole Homer

The Pocketknife Bible — Anis Mojgani

Pole Dancing to Gospel Hymns — Andrea Gibson

Racing Hummingbirds — Jeanann Verlee

Reasons to Leave the Slaughter — Ben Clark

Redhead and the Slaughter King — Megan Falley

Rise of the Trust Fall — Mindy Nettifee

Said the Manic to the Muse — Jeanann Verlee

Scandalabra — Derrick C. Brown

Slow Dance with Sasquatch — Jeremy Radin

The Smell of Good Mud — Lauren Zuniga

Some of the Children Were Listening — Lauren Sanderson

Songs from Under the River — Anis Mojgani

Strange Light — Derrick C. Brown

38 Bar Blues — C.R. Avery

This Way to the Sugar — Hieu Minh Nguyen

Time Bomb Snooze Alarm — Bucky Sinister

Uh-Oh — Derrick C. Brown

Uncontrolled Experiments in Freedom — Brian S. Ellis

The Undisputed Greatest Writer of All Time — Beau Sia

The Way We Move Through Water — Lino Anunciacion

We Will Be Shelter — Andrea Gibson, Editor

What Learning Leaves — Taylor Mali

What the Night Demands — Miles Walser

Working Class Represent — Cristin O'Keefe Aptowicz

Workin' Mime to Five — Dick Richards

Write About an Empty Birdcage — Elaina Ellis

Yarmulkes & Fitted Caps — Aaron Levy Samuels

The Year of No Mistakes — Cristin O'Keefe Aptowicz

Yesterday Won't Goodbye — Brian S. Ellis

CPSIA information can be obtained
at www.ICGtesting.com
Printed in the USA
JSHW010750220922
30843JS00004B/21